Prologue

Apologies due from me in this regard since I began this trek a few years ago when I thought someone besides me would give a rat's ass about reading this kind of stuff. I admittedly became disillusioned and lost, misplaced or simply threw away the original works. Everything works out for the best, I suppose. Over the years, I have written small articles, song bits, sayings, quotes, requested or otherwise, and thought of this quest in an attempt to take it a step further. The thought processes mainly were the ramblings of experiences, thoughts and conclusions due to superiors, elders and brethren before me, whether intended or by osmosis. It seemed like a lot of common sense. It's been mainly a fun trip, with side doses of harsh reality; hoping to learn something and pass along; even if at my expense. It's ok. Hey, if you can't laugh at yourself, take criticisms... so the saying goes?

A number of years ago, I was given a plaque by some friends/associates of mine for accomplishments these individuals were able to achieve, in some way due to my extended processes of due diligence given to them. There was no poetic justice in their words, nothing between the lines or hidden meanings; just good wishes for Karen and me. Since that time, I have come to understand how true those words have become from these individuals, even if the event has long past from our thoughts.

1

If these passages give any information, enjoyment, realization or just plain disagreement for anyone, then those who have assisted in these endeavors, I wholeheartedly thank. Since, without their unsuspecting assistance, they have reminded me things do change and life must move along.

I will leave it at that, and let these writings do the rest.

Elmo P. Lugnutt

"Tomorrow is promised to no one, so have fun along the way"

Said by many, practiced by few

Diary of A Retired Mad Man

My Ultimate Level of Dumbfounded Ness

I was having a conversation with my wife Karen one day not too long ago. She said with all the ideas and thoughts permeating in and out of my head, I should start writing them down. I thought about it, and here we go…..

My music iPod is always set on shuffle. My genre range from older jazz to some present rock with blues and other stuff in between because it seems my mood for what I want to hear changes about as frequently as the shuffle. Maybe that's the whole idea. I have always thought I would like to write these things and then I don't follow through.

We've all seen the movie (or real life situation) where the laid off executive figures s/he now has the time to write about their life's work/experiences. Like most of us care. What usually happens (and it seems like it will happen to me at any moment) is after about two or three pages, we either hit the tube or fall asleep. Or just realize we don't have as much to write about as we originally believed.

Besides, who buys all the books you see in the book stores or online anyway? Seems like there are more books than people.

I am presently in a "retired" state, and don't know if it will stay that way forever; but I do enjoy the moments in each day. It's too bad many of us grew up believing we had to follow certain rules of society to get to the age of retirement. Although the government may see to it that things will change regardless of our goals. I had a fairly decent career in the commercial finance business, got two kids (and offered some assistance with three stepsons) through it all. Kids give us some of our greatest moments and disappointments, but that's all I wish to say about this matter.

There was a movie called "Brewster's Millions" about a ball player who had to spend a certain amount of money in a certain period of time to obtain an even greater sum of money. It's not so much the theme of the movie that I relate to as a certain section where Brewster says the candidate of choice in the election scene should be "none of the above". This is where some naivety on my part may come into play. But I believe we need more "none of the above" working for us; so that those who cannot seem to understand that some forms of ambition can truly be the ultimate last resort to failure. Maybe I've just gotten older but why do we constantly place folks in charge who continually make their "temporary positions" a self serving one? Even the president cannot serve more than two terms in a row, so why do the other positions offer a potential working life long scenario?

Oh, I know, we can't get the full "benefit" of the person in charge during such a short tenure.....does the word "bullshit" come to mind? If we as a people cannot find others to fill the shoes of absolute power before it corrupts absolutely, then there is something wrong with us, and we get what we deserve.

It's a good thing I can put these thoughts on hold a little bit, especially when I am taking a break to drive.....

August 7, 2009

My wife said something relating to "it's because you're a man".....I understand this, but already forgot what it was she related the comment....just like a man, I suppose.

Health care, what a trip, eh...? No matter how hard they try to divert this topic, it always comes back...will probably have to reserve judgment here simply because the jury's still out. However, I cannot help but wonder why we need to make wholesale changes for what works for most folks. Some people may simply choose not to have health insurance.

My broker and his son/partner just left the brokerage house they had been at for many years. The son informs me they didn't want to leave, but events led it to happening. I chalk this one up to the "everything eventually changes" in my head department. I will probably follow them to their new home; hoping things will go along as they did at the old home, but who knows.

Read another Tim Dorsey book….god do I wish I could think and write like that….the books aren't for everyone. They are weird by many accounts, but somehow, I'm always drawn to them. I always try to have two or three books going at the same time. I pretty much remember most of what's going on, or read the previous page or two where I left off if I forget.

Another thing about that health care stuff, when they decide to force it on you, and you weigh much more than the charts say, do the police show up at your door from time to time make certain you're not couching out on pork rinds with "light beer"? Can they put a 1984 style camera system in the house? Where will that take us, oh my!!

Think it's time for a cigar out back with my neighbor the Colonel…back later.

August 9, 2009

I just finished watching a Korean War series. It's too bad they don't teach the real history any more. Maybe the meaning would still be lost on the present population. It's everything from bravery to loss of bigotry to comradeship that people have to do at their own expense so a few leaders can save face. A real tragedy as in all wars, but hey, if you don't want what war brings, then don't have'em.

August 10, 2009

My former employer calls and requests I assist in a public sale on some repossessed equipment. I will be paid a fee acceptable to me. In case I have not mentioned, I am, or was in the commercial equipment finance business for over 37 years. I do not know if I will or should see the 38th, as the time in rank has, shall we say, worn me down. But overall the business, which can be stressful at times, was a worthwhile one. There were times, as many of us believe, that we should have done something else, or at least tried something else before 37 years went by, but it never quite happened. This writing thing has always been a bit of a thought of mine over the years, but now that I am "un working" for a living (a term I just made up since the departure was voluntary and as I mentioned earlier, have no idea if or when I will re-enter this line of work) I, with the encouragement of the significant other, decided to give it a whirl. If nothing else, I may get some things resolved in my head and make more peace with myself.

Did I mention I am reading three books at the same time? It is kind of a challenge. I do not know what book I will pick up on any given day, as they are all at various stages. The topics are varied, but usually lean towards comical/historical fiction (Tim Dorsey novels about Florida antics; the stuff he writes, man, it is funny and so much, while fictional in character, is true about much of the state. You'd have to live here a long time like me (over 30 years and traveled it) to know. You have to know a lot of folks and/or do lots of research to write and/or have folks assist you to write a lot of this stuff.

August 11, 2009

I held the sale for my former employer. Pretty routine, except somehow the camera "lost" the photographs I took of the equipment. Oh, well, tomorrow's another one. Another saying I have heard of late is "If you believe you can or you can't, you're right". I like it. Sayings used to be something I remembered more, whether they were in songs (in between the moon and you, angels get a better view of the crumbling difference between wrong and right) or just plain old ones I made up (there's no such thing as a quick question). They are cute, but I wonder how many of us adhere to them, especially under stress, anger and/or frustration. Like we see children who have had tough lives with medical problems and say, "I don't really have it bad", but then forget about not really having it that bad when bad things seem to happen.

I spoke with Karen about the lost photograph problem. She was making suggestions I already tried and when she asked if I tried another way, I got flustered, let her know I would probably just try to get more photos tomorrow and hung up. I tried to call back a few minutes later to see if there was anything towards getting upset. No answer. I did eventually get her on the third try. No animosity. Maybe it was just my imagination.

August 13, 2009

This health care issue: I believe the horse may be out of the barn, so to speak, so it seems no matter what Congress does, there will probably be very little trust. Buried deep in the way-too-many-page-albeit-not- yet-adopted documents are items pertaining to how Congress folk will not be subject to the same laws as the rest of us. Our lawmakers says things (when they can get a word in edgewise) that the American people don't understand or the town meeting attendees are not the representation of the people....one question to them.....uhhhh, like,....what planet are they on? They don't even read what is given to them, don't pay attention when someone actually tries to speak intelligently (taking cell phone calls) and claim everything's a set up because they know what's best and just "take our word for it, you won't get screwed". This is not new news, but I wonder, how many cases does an attorney have to lose to become a politician? Or how many failed businesses or bad checks or illegalities of an array of items does it take for one's own ultimate failure to become one of our elected officials? If you think they just started having all these problems after they took office, I have this bridge I would like to sell you. They don't have any skin in the game.

August 19, 2009

Took a break for a few days. Things are pretty slow. I asked around on the business cycle but not much happening. What creative juices I can muster at times for my skill level don't always come to the surface or,.....oops, I just had one of those senior moments...went blank again. At least that's all I hope it is......I think I will download some CD's into the computer to transfer to the IPod. I figured out if you capitalize letters like "CD" and IPod", the computer recognizes them and you don't get that nasty little red line under the typing indicating a potentially misspelled word. Guess it recognizes the new age terminology.

August 21, 2009

Later today, I am having lunch with an old business associate and friend of many years. Most of my friends/associates are moved away or retired. A few have passed on. Things change, and while it is good to hold onto history, for where would we be without it, embracing the new, or at least a portion of it, can be rewarding as well. C'est la vie, or whatever the future holds, mostly we cannot predict, only react to it. Sometimes I do not do well with it, but I think I'm getting better. You would have to ask my wife, as she is a truly independent observer. Most of us do not like change. The minor nuances of change which can be "merged" into our thought processes become acceptable.

August 25, 2009

I have been in contact with several of the folks in my former profession. Things don't seem so good yet; and it will take time. But the market is just in that mode right now. One of my old reps working for another company the last few years, says they are trying to obtain audited financials, not only for bonding purposes, but for DOT certification to be able to work on jobs where the supposed TARP money went (for those of you who care and not in the know, that's Troubled Asset Relief Program). I find it interesting that my rep's company has to go through hoops to be close to the funds of folks who probably couldn't do the work they do in the first place. It's like inspectors who couldn't run their own companies but get to tell the folks who do own firms how they're going to be treated. I'll leave it there.

The business we chose to be in for many years is becoming unrecognizable. Maybe it's for the best. Things do change. Or maybe we just got old and it's more the same than different, only older eyes don't see it that way. Someone said today that adults are obsolete children. We lose the ability to see things in a new light. Does that doom us, or just put us further back on the shelf? Break time again…

August 27, 2009

The power went out for about three hours. I just realized this written document seems like a big diary. I didn't want it to sound that way. Maybe some books read that way, but none that I have read come to mind. I am irritable today. Maybe this retirement sometimes makes me think too much. I keep busy about half the day and tend to daydream for a bit, but I suppose it's a routine. The colonel wants to smoke a cigar down by the lake this afternoon. It's something I usually look forward to, because not many of the folks I know are in the "scotch or beer with a decent cigar" mode. Besides, he's a walking history book and I enjoy the conversation.

These czars of this administration, holy shit, I mean. I heard one talk yesterday. Talk about reverse discrimination. I suppose they believe two wrongs make a Wright (no sorry, I don't mean the reverend, just "right"). I don't know where this is all going to lead, but normal Democrats/Liberals would blush over this stuff (I am a card carrying chicken independent with a certain mean streak about it type). Maybe it's time to ditch the parties and have folks say what they mean and mean what they say. After all, if the only reason one would disagree with someone's opinion is because they are in the opposite camp..... But it could still come to violence if we are not careful.

August 28, 2009

Too many banks are obtaining all the necessary capital from the government to go back to the same old problems they started in the first place. The choices for pure capitalism (that means freedom) are starting to narrow, and so what if the oligopoly tightens its grip on smaller institutions, as long as the government has a say in how the money flows. Not a big institution fan myself, many of these banks needed to come down to earth, and I mean hard, because how much worse would it have been for the real backbone of the county, small businesses, to obtain funds if they fail? For that matter, giving all companies a free tax bill for the year would have saved most of the stimulus money from ever having to be printed, but that's not how you maintain control.

Earlier today I heard someone say "you can't make a weak man strong by making a strong man weak". Something Abraham Lincoln once said. Interesting how those quotes don't seem to make it when the majority of folks have what they need and like and we want to turn everything upside down for the minority of folks who can't, or won't or do not even choose to obtain health care.

I have added another book to my repertoire of items called "Eye on the Prize". It was written many years ago by Juan Williams, a respected contributor to Fox news and other Washington area associations. I have not read many pages yet, but again, if we are speaking about those who, by their own efforts to succeed or prosper in their own constitutionally allowed free ways are hampered by those who would stop them because of the color of skin, I say those who stop these folks are parasites. The problem comes along when folks who want a piece of the pie for nothing. For them, this book would teach them nothing. People who would yell "it's our time now!!"….well, it depends on who's the "our". More than likely, the "our" mentioned here are not the deserved ones, because the ones who truly believe it is their time (or your or my time for that matter) do-not-have-to-advertise-it!! The laws of the land were written for all to follow and prosper, not for individual(s) to change the laws to suite the needs of the few, especially those most undeserving. I will have to read more to understand further. The book takes its turn with the others I read concurrently, and I read slowly, but I am not in a hurry, knowing since history has been written, it will be patient.

August 29, 2009

I am sitting out back with Karen, staring at the sky while she reviews her bibles (cookbooks). Looking up …. there are no perfect places, only perfect moments. I'm in one. The Navy boys are playing this morning out of Key West. Jets chasing each other above, practicing keeping us safe, I hope. Waving to folks rowing by in the lake, the faint smell of cigar in the air (probably in the shirt I was wearing last night and put on again this morning). The neighborhood cat comes by through the old cat door left from our old cat days.

I am listening to Joe Jackson on the IPod. Getting ready to pick weeds, it doesn't get much better. She thinks it doesn't get better for me either. I told her a friend of mine e-mailed me yesterday, asking how I was doing. I respond in kind, and his response is, based on my current situation vs. his, "you are the wind beneath my wings" or however that crummy song goes. Karen howls after I tell her. I find no humor in making me the butt end of words in crummy songs (only kidding).

We had to get off the news and WSJ stuff I read earlier this morning. Somehow, there seems to be some folk who believe the only people who really exist in this world leave the borders of New York and once they cross it, they think they're in California, like there's nothing in between.

August 30, 2009

Karen and I went out to dinner last night. A small order of mussels and soup with a few Dewar's and soda always softens the day. The conversation I had with her about the broker's optimism about the market was mostly, but not totally, by me. Like the state of the state of Florida, I called it a "false positive" (this must be a good one because Karen really liked my assessment on this one, if not from the broker argument but of the state one).

Here's how it goes. Most everyone understands or hears about the basic underlying problems we face today; and with enough negatives opposing enough positives, maybe you understand where the falsehoods about recovery lies, at least for now. On the state of the state, let's face it, for years before the mid to late 20th century, what was Florida but a place for wealthy folks to come and escape the cold? Then along comes the "conditioning of air", add to this some guy who invented a better mouse trap few years earlier, buys land to create a "rat kingdom" of sorts, and voila!!.....instant middle class flocking to a place they have no idea about!

Anyway, getting back to the false positive here. I have a theory that after all these folks came here over the last 50-60 years; the place would now start to suffer (to the delight of some) a declining population base. Add a decent storm or two to the mix, coupled with insurance company flight (fright), and people will start moving to build better places to live in cooler climates. As I mentioned earlier somewhere above, there are no perfect places, only perfect moments, and we may have to reassess when those moments will come.

September 2, 2009

I was born and raised in The Bronx. No, everything I learned did not come from playing in the concrete jungles they called the playgrounds, but looking back, there is a lot of irony. The politicians who would either help or hurt you back then would probably be the same types who would do the same to you today. The new administration called for transparency, and we have it. Folks who are or were part of underground movements, bombers and communists seem to be all over the place, proud of their accomplishments.

We take too much blame. Sure, we have had moments out of the sun, but who hasn't. As for "finally being proud to be an American", well how in the hell did we get here, in spite of all the problems, and not be as proud? I believe the racial divide is more evident than ever, and if we do not stop it, the gains which have been achieved are going down the toilet. Look, you cannot regulate attitude (or at least not yet) and nothing is 100 per cent, so take your best posture, vote and let the people decide, otherwise the witch hunt will continue. Most of the ancestors of our previous generations weren't even here when the issues surrounding race become evident. Back to the Bronx times, we grew up will a decent racial mixture even in the fifties, and I'll tell you, the only arguments we mainly had in the school yards, which albeit sometimes came to fights, were where he was "out!" or "safe!" at the base. Disagreements today mean you're a racist. To the very folks who say this, I say "now who's being racist?"

September 3, 2009

It's one of those days, a little weary and my eyes don't work so well. I have been trying to read and keep my ear to the ground on the market. An old customer calls for financing on an amount that may be too small. I cannot seem to get some follow up information for another deal. I seem to be doing a lot pro bono, but it's ok. The long weekend approaches. Nothing in particular is being planned, which is usually the way I prefer things.

I left word for my parents to call. Sometimes it's hard when you're the last man standing, so to speak. Of the three children on my father's side and eight on my mother's, they are the only ones left. After over 62 years of marriage, it has been long in the tooth for them. Mom does not converse well, repeating herself and fusses way too much with her hair. Dad does not handle their discussions well, and they won't change. No computers, barely the voice mail on the phone, no cell phones; I suppose eventually we all succumb to not wanting to join in to new world things. I can only hope after watching them I get a wiser for it, although I have deficiencies my kids will hopefully learn to avoid. My parents probably never thought they would have a 61 year old son telling them to at least try a little. I don't really try too hard because they are who they are, and I do not wish to interfere. I will try to call again.

September 7, 2009

I am dumbfounded by all these new medical prescriptions advertised. They seem to have more side effects than advantages. I suppose they may assist a small percentage of the population, but I suspect when patents run low, companies either have to push the new stuff or buy a company whose patents have a long way to go. As Karen knows I will say at times "that's my (stubborn?) opinion and I'm stickin' to it".

I have ideas. One of my latest came to me when I had to visit a baby factory outlet because we were trying to get something for one of the grandkids birthday. The place was huge, with large lofty ceilings. I reviewed the faces of "what's the use"…
men walking the strollers while moms were doing the things they do in these places. Obviously, the men wished they were elsewhere. So I thought, why not use all the space above by building a sports bar? I mean, let's face it, the women are going to drive when they leave the place, so the guys can go do the sports/drinking thing and everyone knows where everyone is….think about it.

I read an article this morning about a bank I have been asked to join in some advisory way. It would be great part time work, but I don't think it would be part time. If I had to start wearing ties again after all these years…..Karen says I'm thinking about it too much. We'll know soon enough. I think she's jealous I exited the work scene before she did, no?

September 9, 2009

Well, I took the "part-time-full-time" scenario at the bank, so this should fill up a little more of the day. We will try to create something from scratch. It should be interesting, although I don't feel the same rush I did when we created the old branch in the original company from almost nothing. This may hamper my writing time, but we'll see.

Seems the government has enough of its own problems on a regular basis. I heard someone say this morning the left side media will do anything to avert confrontation which will demean the historic nature of this administration, i.e. this President. I believe that attitude, especially where just criticism is justifiable, is demeaning in of itself. To turn a blind eye to things that are wrong, or will keep future generations in debt ad infinitum just to satisfy a hard core of those who think the color of one's skin should give them a pass is, well, wrong. No one in their right mind wants any president to fail in his or her efforts, so when you take out the highs and lows (or in this case the far ends of the politicos), evaluate the damage and control it. No, not 100 percent, because nothing will satisfy 100 percent of the people 100 percent of the time, but what the generally elected representatives are supposed to do. I suspect many of these representatives feel as the people they represent do, but forget about this when it comes to voting on issues because they affect other issue. They vote in a vacuum, and that has dire consequences.

From my own perspective, on the main issue of health care, there have been many ways to try and make it as universal as possible. In the end, I believe the numbers will bring us to our knees is we go forward. I know this can be a difficult thing for those in need, but how you would ultimately keep the government from have a competitive advantage down the line, no matter what the program, seems incongruous to me. They will never have to deal with the same coverage issues as the general populace (that exclusion was supposedly even written in the original 600 or 1300 or whatever page numbered bills) and most will be long gone from their government positions by the time everything hits the fan.

September 11, 2009

It's my first week at trying to reinvent the business I spent my working life in at the bank. It's a bit of an uphill battle and I don't know how excited I feel about it. Not as much as I would have when I was younger, it seems. I do not know how it will go at this early stage. As I said before, "If you think you can or you can't, you're right". God, I hope I don't always have to practice what I speak of here.

Anyway, the health debate goes on. All sides struggling for their rights not to be trampled on. It's a tough situation when there's very little, if any, trust in DC. You know, my limited imagination today says there's not a whole lot more to say about it from above to today's notes, you just get tired of no attention to the matter because it's not in this or that group's political interest. Hopefully, the majority will seize the day. It's time to move on to more pressing issues.

September 14, 2009

As long as I am writing a story about a potential transaction for the bank, I may as well go down a few icons and add some commentary here. It is too early to tell how this venture with the bank will turn out. After all, who are we kidding? The only reason this ideal has merit is because my CEO/President friend/associate of the bank, whom I have known for over 30 years and worked with in Florida when I first arrived, thinks it may have some merit. Under the guise of diversification, we shall try to add some iron to the bank books. Again, this may be too early, but my gut tells me it's not something the other bankers could give a shit about. I can't say I blame them. If I get any deals in front of whatever committee, we'll see where it goes. In the meantime, I am not going crazy driving all over the place; mainly locally and coming home to work in the afternoons rather than go back downtown. That office is so quiet, when I use the telephone, it seems so loud. I suppose everyone else is e-mailing away.

September 16, 2009

Another day around town, more hope than promise so far, but it's way too early in the game. Well, I didn't know we had so many racists in this country, but all these pundits seem to have nothing else to say when, hey, they have nothing else to stand on. I swear, if the president told me that one and one equaled three, and I disagreed, someone would call me a racist, and, as I have mentioned earlier, is getting uglier by the moment. It's a great country still, so we can only hope that common sense will ultimately prevail, and common sense things get done. When you consistently tell people what the have to do because "they don't know any better", you are going to push a snake into a corner, and then the fangs will be exposed. People will do some things because they have to, like work, and hopefully get as much fulfillment out it as they can, but after that, it's because they mainly want to do things. If you reverse the process, the fangs, oh those fangs........

September 22, 2009

It's been a few days since my last thoughts. There have been many, but not worth the writing time. This will probably happen a lot. I'm trying to get straight in my head about this new venture I am involved and admittedly not totally sold on the idea. Sometimes depression comes, but it usually just lingers a little bit because when you get like this, other negatives come into play. You think you can ignore things and they'll just go away, but they don't unless you confront them. You figure you could outlast them, and sometimes you do. I think if you try and settle with things, even if you didn't want to compromise as much as you may have in the settling manner, it brings peace, and you can go on.

September 23, 2009

I am back already.

I watched Mr. Beck and others last evening and this morning (only 6:16 am or so now). If you are like minded and rational with most of our American brethren, you just sometimes get tired of "IT": I do not mean that we shouldn't care because god knows, the politicians like nothing better than apathy so they can go about their ultimate goal of the status quo of really getting nothing done but getting re-elected. By "IT", I mean with all the ways to blog, or twitter or look up the "facts", it's about as difficult to ascertain truth that when we were more in the dark. It's like we're even more in the dark, just with a lot more head spinning facts. Pick something you feel passionate about, and go for it, lest you drive yourself crazy. Just remember that while you should fight for your opinions, it may not be the whole truth, or the only one. I think some Chinese fellow said that a long time ago.

September 24, 2009

Just thinking about something my insurance company sent to me not too long ago. It seems there is a possibility the company will be closing some of its branches and a letter comes from the agency saying if I like my agency I should vote that I love them on certain questions. It isn't that I have any beef in particular, but it is interesting to note the divisional company of the parent will soon be sold to another agency. Once the surviving agency's move on to the other company, whether mine survives or otherwise, it will be interesting to see how much more the policy will cost to maintain to cover the costs of the sale. You see, whether my agency stays open or not, the policy holders finance the sale even though no claims may be made during the period. God forbid you have a claim during that period. It's just another example of big government/business scenarios. We help the agency and it still costs us.

September 25, 2009

The Federal Reserve says they see signs things are picking up. Maybe they need to put down their protractors and calculators and step outside for awhile. Maybe the reason for the slowdown in unemployment and layoffs and housing problems is because we've just about squeezed everything we can from these areas and when some indicator goes up, it is still a gazillion points below where is was a day, week, month or year ago. Ok, ok, enough of the negativity. Anything that happens in a positive light today will take time to work its way into the mainstream. I visited a vendor today (like most, no outside assistance to greet me, all laid off) who said they were closing their parts store in another city. The rate of slowdown slows down, but how long before they feel confident to open that parts store again? Do they factor in the cost of the parts going and coming from this site to the contractors' jobsites? What if the contractor makes the longer trip to this site vs. the shorter distance to the now defunct parts store? Does the vendor give the contractor a price break for added downtime away from the job? I like this; put down your protractor so you can get with your contractor can figure it out....this, and many other questions will be answered in the next chapter of .....S-O-A-P.....sorry a little brevity in the head for those who remember the sitcom.....

September 29, 2009

Not much to write about of late. The loan committee at the bank meets today to review something I conjured up with an old customer (really a real loan request) for a credit line. I am still not totally on board in my head with this gig, but I hope it will change for me. Who knows; let's face it, I am what I am. I tell myself, "get up, dress up and show up"; any maybe that helps make the day, or at least part of it.

September 30, 2009

Listening to one of my favorite tunes of many in the jazz world called "Lush Life" on the way to the store. Playing is John Coltrane, but I also enjoy other versions of it from Joe Henderson and Chet Baker. I wish I could live by this lush life we have all the time, because in America, that's what it's all about. I hope it stays that way. Sure, everyone says we have problems, but boy, some of them are so obvious we're crazy to take it anymore.....anyway, I didn't want to go there now, just enjoyed the tunes (which is all I listen to in the car, no news or "squawk" radio)....just the tunes, if you please.

October 1, 2009

Fall!!!....really been a little cooler last day or so. After many years here, I get into a May to October funk. I don't mind the heat all that much, and if you live here, well, there isn't much you can do about it anyway, except to stay indoors if it bugs you enough (that is, of course, if you're a/c doesn't give you problems from time to time, but that's another story). I was informed by committee the other day most of the work I would be doing in the job was not going to materialize.... bummer. Now, it becomes even more part time, but, one day at a time, eh?

Karen's been sick. A first timer on the puke meter, but if you're eating now, that's more than you want to know. The news.....the news, it's a concern. So many things so obviously wrong, so many egos are in the mix, and no one wants to let go....someone once said "at the feast of ego, everyone leaves hungry"... It's too bad, because the majority takes it in the shorts over the issues, but somehow, life goes on. Even while we are blind-sided, life...goes...on.

I went out for awhile today calling on customers, as what I normally do during the week. They all seem to have the same problems, i.e. not enough or very little business. I have a feeling this will not end anytime soon, and although I may say the turn will come sometime next year, I wonder about that timeframe for many. I have lost many customers to attrition, simple retirement/going out of business, or death. The ones which remain will have to do business in a different manner from a lending standpoint. More information required, more time to approve (or reject) deals and more stringent terms. This may not be helpful to the vendors when it does turn, but at least they'll know of where I am coming. I suppose when you take out the highs and lows, this change was inevitable. I have tried to teach myself to respect the past, and embrace the future, lest you don't want one. It is not always so easy, but I try.

October 6, 2009

You know, it's incredible what some people will do or say when they get in front of a TV camera. Makes you wonder what you or I would say, especially if it happened enough or you simply missed it from a time before. It must be a mystical thing, because what comes out of peoples mouths could not have be given much thought prior to speaking. News flash.....there really isn't any right or left wind type conspiracies going on, and no, most folks don't care about the color of one's skin when it comes themselves being skinned alive over the crap many media pun dents are trying to push. Enough of them, be it from the Hollywood self indulgent crowd to those craving to be just like them (there is no right or wrong, just what I say must be the truth) just can't help

29

themselves, and we, the indulgent group, have to compromise, forgive, forget and go on. Bull.

Karen and I took a Sunday "off" from the norm to go do things away for the day. What we did was not as important as doing it, because we did not read the paper or listen to the news and when you lose track of the day to day events, not being informed is, well, not so bad. Guess what, you're still alive to get back to life's events the next day if you so choose, but didn't it feel great, no medications (save those at the barstool) no bad feelings and no one to yell at you over how you can sit there and do nothing when the country's going down the toilet.....it felt great.

The only reason the country may indeed feel like it's slipping away it because we are allowing it slip into the stage of from apathy to dependence on others who would sell us out anyway. While we sit and debate and play nice, those who will not continue to goose step their way down the path. It's been done before and we all know the outcome, only the stakes are higher, and the destruction will be quicker, deadlier, and draw more players into the arena. Heaven, God, or whatever you believe, help us if it gets to that point.

October 7, 2009

Income redistribution.....another phrase we keep hearing about these days. Let's try and give it some fairness. When I think back on all the crap I learned in high school.....well, no, maybe another time, but I wasn't the sharpest crayon in the box back in school. The counselors, maybe trying to be well meaning in their own way, might have well been accused of "steerage". That is, you're probably not good enough to get into this college or that school (grades notwithstanding), so maybe a trade school, or better yet, the military. They would post names of the seniors and all the schools they got accepted. Back then, we didn't think of it as a humiliation or demeanor of character, or at least not outwardly. By today's standards, the lawyers would be setting up shop in the school corridors.

In any event, what the well-intentioned guidance folks were trying to impress upon some folks (and Karen agrees and has brought this up with me before) is that maybe, just maybe, an academic college is not the best suited option for some, or more than just some (again, money to afford, scholarships and grades aside). The folk's best equipped to assist in one's life endeavors may not always be your parents. They're scared to death. They're scared because if you don't become a doctor, lawyer or Indian chief, how you gonna' survive, eh? I realize they're supposed to have your best interests in mind, and their input should be valid and a part of the thinking of the future process, but the final decisions should be made the individual whose life has to be lived, and with the happiest possible pursuits.

I tried to listen to the experts in my case. I would be the first to go to college, after a stint in a computer school (the stuff we learned in the Smithsonian, of course). I would pay for school myself, work and go to school days and nights. It was a… lotta' fun. I would also be the first in the family to get drafted! But that's another story.

I guess the point I should get back to is the administration seems to feel they have to tax the piss out of those who already pay hefty sums into the system, which still seems to stifle competition and prohibit growth and trade. If we mean we try and see if more folks coming up in the pipeline towards would care to be in the sciences, technologies and trades, then we would feel more inclined to understand the balance we are trying to achieve. Careers that don't create, just shuffle paper from one entity to another just creates too much incentive to manipulate, as we have all seen of late. I told a banker friend of mine not too long ago that his business should be a boring business (I may have indicated this before). Once you got away from the boredom (risky trading, insurance, collateralized debt obligations, etc.) you lose your soul, and I don't necessarily mean it in religiously, for I am not of that vein. I mean your consciousness. You become disingenuous. Anyone with any understanding of this would have a hard time looking in the mirror. After all, how much money do you really need to live? Translation….less lawyers and bank executives with narrow focus, more of the brains towards innovation.

October 9, 2009

Let's face it, when it comes right down to it, there's an "old?" saying, "who do you trust, Washington or yourself?" 'Tis a sham, or shame what they do with our money, and I would be damned if we had to give them anymore than they are "legally" entitled. I had some interesting thoughts about this earlier in the day, but I was driving and they popped in and now they are gone. I don't really hate when that occurs, maybe because it's part of the body's cleansing process, to keep one sane. The line of thought had something to do with how with all the competition in the world today, other countries, while trying to condemn us, will also try to emulate us, or at least what we used to be, unless we take back what is ours.

October 13, 2009

Toby Keith sings about "The Angry American", and I thought it was pretty good. This is about what this country has created from its inception. Sure, there are bleak moments in the relatively short history in comparison to some other countries, but those who would condemn us the loudest only need to look back at their own histories and sit down. When you're on top of the heap, it's easy have stones thrown at one target. I hope we prevail, but there are forces out there with differing opinions and again, that may not be such at bad thing, as long as it is out in the open, to avoid as much suspicion and corrupt ways of doing things as possible. Is that possible? We shall see.

October 15, 2009

Wall street bank/brokerage houses to make record profits i.e. bonuses even after they pay back the taxpayer monies they shouldn't have received in the first place......health care to cost so much more than the "game show hosts" (I stole that one from Sting, listen to "If I Ever Lose My Faith In You") will ever say....media pendants (sluts) making up things people didn't say, but suits their ratings.....making nice with our real enemies in the world, getting a "piece of the pie" prize and sending more folks off to war.....economists (who probably listen to Wall street folks) saying the recession/depression is over and news folks blah, blahing it out because, well, the economists say so (not all, though)...unemployment, the excessive printing of money (although many countries are guilty of same).......change we can believe in?....

October 16, 2009

If everyone in the world were exactly the same color, I mean to the point where there would be no difference, then we'd be open to racial discussion about the size of your nose, or the way certain people's eyebrows go up, or the color of hair......it's just our nature, I suppose.

October 20, 2009

1502 pages, according to what I heard this morning.....1502
pages......how long will it take a congressperson to read this
piece of.....of ......legislature?....do the math....an average
reader, which I assume they are.....about a week. Hell, they
can't hold their attention on anything that long......who
writes this stuff and why so long?....so the lawyers think they
can cover the bases (they'll find a way to sue anyway)....or is
it a more sinister plot?.....I suspect much of this waste of trees
has more to do with camouflage and less to do with trying not
to eventually tax you on these matters. After all, most folks
involved will be long gone by the time you feel this pain.

No cost of living increase to you on the most grandiose Ponzi
scheme ever, but them congress folks just got more dough for
themselves...awwww, what the hell, this is all old
stuff.....just vote everyone out........unfortunately, this
pyramid is paying into far more "worthy" causes (hoping you
won't die from tainted water supplies so you can collect),
then for this schemes original intentions.

October 22, 2009

You know, it's a good thing "Married with Children" reruns
are on when I get up on the weekday mornings or the news
would drive you crazy. I am certain most of us are fairly sick
of politicos saying "when you said it, it wasn't a good idea,
but because we brought it up now, it seems like a pretty good

one".....people's livelihoods as well as their lives are at stake here, and politicians are concerned about looking good. Now, I will go find something meaningful to do.

October 27, 2009

Another day, been nothing new, nothing gained, no new perspective kinda' time it seems....need some fulfillment, although just not watching the news should be enough....still too naïve to understand why a government wants to do so much for those who will not do for themselves.....control. It's the only "public option" I can understand. When it comes down to it, you voice your opinion, vote, let democracy takes its course, and move on with the verdict. In the laws of the universe (and I will quote and/or use from time to time here)...where you go, wherever you end up...there you are....enjoy.

November 4, 2009

November, they say already or something like that....not much changed from last week. Weather's getting a little cooler, time for a change.

November 5, 2009

The greater good.....you ever notice how when some things
hit the spotlight, that it seems to be about one person or a
small group of folks who do not represent the norm (whatever
that means, and no, not the Norm of Cheers fame, although
that isn't a bad analogy) seem to try and tip the balance in
their favor with the assistance of others who like the control.
It seems there's a lot of the "tail wagging the dog" situations
these days, and while I understand human nature can play a
part of this in anyone's life, the greater good should always
be examined as the best alternative. I was going to site two
examples that occurred recently, one if sports and the other,
you guessed it, politics/health care, but the point is, it should
not be happening, at least at the magnitude it is occurring.

November 13, 2009

Another week plus break since nothing much to report most
of us haven't heard enough already. We can't call a murderer
in the name of Allah for what he is, a terrorist Muslim
murderer....there, I said it because that is what it
is.......wouldn't you call a Mafia hit done by an Italian if
that's who did it? We need to get over the stereotype.....most
Italians aren't in the mafia and most Muslims are not
terrorists. Next topic, please.

It's really amazing when I read stories about the times folks
get a chance to corral a congress person and ask fair and

sometimes tough questions, mainly relating to "how are we going to pay for it", whatever topic "it" may be…..in many cases, as it relates to health insurance. Tea party goers are no good unsavory people who would harass and talk and act violently (no evidence there, by the way). Yet you get congress folks backed into a corner because you ain't buyin' the BS anymore, and watch who tries to get nasty. They are out of options folks, but it's still gonna' cost us. Vote them far away next time, if you please. They know you can never tax and spend your way into prosperity, the only means to an end here is an attempt to control more folks' lives. It ain't over yet, I just don't think we're gonna' take it anymore. You think these congress types are not going to let illegals get as much if not more rights than legals, or that congress folks are going to be covered under the same government plan they think they can stuff down our throats……..but now, on to more burning questions, like, who was the lazy ass that invented the remote control, and even more pressing, how do you get all the little pieces of paper you just shredded into the garbage bag without getting any on the floor? What's even more amazing is where I will find those little scrapings days later after I thought I got them all.

November 17, 2009

It was a great day to be out and about in Florida weather wise. The car windows down on the local roads, looking up to the mostly blue sky, a smattering of clouds, the Navy boys playing the fly pattern good-guy-bad-guy games streaking through the heavens. I always assume they do these things on nice days so the lines can be seen by many. If Armageddon ever arrives, it would probably have to be on a day like today. After all, no nut case could be happy without being able to see and have others observe the mushroom clouds in the sky, and that just wouldn't work on a cloudy day.

Karen probably thinks I am a little nuttier now, especially after eventually reading excerpts like the one above. She's a good egg, putting up with my mood swings. She may never understand how much it means for me to have her around, but I hope she does. We have become more private in recent times, Voltaire's "be civil to all, cordial to many and familiar with few" verse becoming more evident and important in these days. Sometimes it's just better not to know too many folks too well. As long as we respect other's space, enjoy the company of others on occasion and don't ask too many questions about the past (a cocktail or two and a decent cigar never hurt either), I'm good.

November 20, 2009

"Woefully misguided"....that's the term I read today about folks who believe spending our way to prosperity's going to save us......obviously, these folks were either not good at math, never owned or controlled a business where profit and loss needs to be managed or are thinking of (or actually) getting something out of going along with this spending. It's too bad, because simple tax/payroll type cuts, the simplest thing this simple minded one can think of, would go a long way to helping out, but hey, that's too easy and, of course, the government can't control matters if they simply do things which make common sense.

December 11, 2009

Whaddaymean, I don't have anything much to do? I spend most of the time deleting the incoming junk e-mails then unsubscribing because I no longer want them ....well, that's a living, isn't it?

February 24, 2010

Apparently I am the one woefully misguided. I must be, because most of the media outlets will tell us how "ig-nant" we are because we don't agree with the politicos. That's why we put them there, because they were supposed to represent us, so and if we want to change things, we need to kill them off (voting wise, not really kill them) or something like that and replace with others. I believe that is beginning to occur. A president who, we are told, hangs pictures of himself all over the place.....Karen and I still cannot figure what he accomplished to get where he is, but if it was anything like winning a peace prize, then we understand.

Spending has gone wild, and I fear it will come back to haunt us unless some form or group of folks know something we do not. I have had a lot of time to read lately, latest book American Lion, story of Andrew Jackson. Pretty good but slow to read. He seemed a very decent president, hated the British and Indians to a racist degree, if that would be the term of the day. Sometimes even great individual do evils of their time, but that would be in many others cultures as well. It doesn't mean great things weren't accomplished to get this country where it is today. I hear Indians don't like twenty dollar bills for exchange in their casinos if at all possible. It's still in reading process, so we'll see where it goes, but we don't seem to have folks like this anymore. This could be because we don't teach this kind of history anymore (or ever, in some cases, worrying too much about being politically correct). We do what we do for the times, and sometimes, just sometimes, you end up with something called America, and we try to correct past mistakes, make the best of it, and move on.

It's too bad it has to come to so much meanness. I mean, I received some photos in an e-mail passed along, the woman in the photo purportedly being Mr. O'bama's mother. The photos are old, and she would appear to be in compromising positions. Now, while I may not agree a lot with what Mr. O'bama is doing, why do we continually have to pass this stuff around? I say purportedly, because who knows if it is really her, and if it is, this stuff should stop. Sometimes things occurred in my career that made me wish I did something else for a living, but the folks who have to transverse in this minefield, on both sides of the aisle, jeezzz, go do some good out there instead of this stuff. I just don't care about it. Discuss the merits of the person and the ideas brought forth; leave this stuff to children, because that is what we look like when we have to resort to these passages. I deleted the photos.

March 7, 2010

I've been reading more history of late, about the other side of capitalism, some history of Russia, Marx, Lenin and the big winner of the slaughter game, Stalin. I found some of what Marx thought to be of some value, depending on the country and bourgeoisie vs. proletarian chasms being affected at a given time in a country's history. I have heard before you have to at least try and understand what your opponent's type of thinking is all about. They certainly spent their lifetimes achieving some pretty impressive, if not horrific things. When Stalin said "when one person dies, it is a tragedy, when a million die, it is a statistic", (a million would have been at least a lower indicator, since the final tally coming in these days is many more times that number) was he referring to the death of his wife at a young age, thus depriving any real feelings towards his brethren? We can never know.

When compared to some of the tests against today arguments in this country, I cannot find much common ground. Socialists claim that capitalism has brought this country to the brink of a new age, and the only way is more and more government. I believe had the government stepped aside and let some of the banks, brokerage houses, insurance companies, and auto industry take its normal capitalistic course rather than bail them out, they may have failed, and it may have been painful, but I wonder how much more investment the rank and file who saved their whole lives for a decent retirement would have lost in that scenario. At least there may have been some comfort in the knowledge while we may have lost as much of our wealth, the folks who helped do this in the first place wouldn't have been bailed out. Still, people in these arenas lost jobs, and part of the blame will always rest with the rank and file, since we did some pretty moronic things to live beyond our means. It's not death and destruction yet, but as we continue to spend away, at some point, financial destruction can take as devastating effect as any.

In one of the scenes in The Godfather, Michael is in the basement with Clemenza practicing with the gun he will use in the restaurant. The families will probably "go to the mattresses" over the result of Michael's objective and he asks Clemenza how bad did he think it would be. Clemenza says something to the effect of "pretty bad, but you know these things have to happen every five-ten years or so, it cleans out the bad blood" (give or take on the paraphrasing here). In other words, like capitalism, when things get too out of line, unimpeded by government or any other interventions, the problems will weed themselves out, the bad elements are left to falter and fail on there own, and the market goes on.

March 22, 2010

Well, now we have it. In some way, shape or form, the health care package is on its way to passage. There will be more government control, which will lead to more inflation, which will lead to more money printing, but only for a little while. When the ends don't justify the means, the spending will abruptly stop; more states will fall in line with California's free fall, and everything the forefathers fought not to do will have been for naught. Remember, I am speaking from an opinion, and if you do not share this opinion and think it is better for a "nanny state", and then we are at odds. At least we'll have that to disagree upon and be allowed to dispute in a free society. I hope.

The IRS will enforce the "tax" on health insurance, and we'll probably have to free a few more murderers and such so we can make room for the abundance of "tax cheats" which will clog the prisons. No more freedom to succeed or fail (oh, and you failures, don't be a hypocrite if it comes to that and look for government help, unless they owed it to you in the first place). God knows, even if it's due you (all the Social Security taxes), you don't really believe it will be there. Private pensions, a luxury the company says will enhance your retirement income, was a pact you made with a supposedly healthy company at the time to forgo additional monies at raise time (assuming you got or deserved one) so you could collect it at a later date, presumably at retirement. Many of those pensions have gone by the wayside, in some cases not so much because the company terminated them due to economics, but because under the guise of economical reasons, the monies were systematically raided by those who thought they deserved it more than the rank and file.

March 24, 2010

So now we have children, supposedly without the knowledge of their parent(s), parading around in public areas touting for more welfare benefits. It has to start as young as possible because these would be the future progressives who keep the present ones in power. No free thinking individual, living every day working hard for themselves and families, would ever want someone else to take care of their needs. How much more basic does it need to be explained? You either take care of yourself, or, barring injury making one incapable of doing so themselves (opened a can of worms here?), you're fan of the European style nanny state. Even in Europe these days, some countries are seeing they cannot support an aging populace with less people coming on line in the workplace.
It's wrong to accept it, in my opinion, but the very folks who will claim to help you only want you to feed off them for support, continuing their never ending control.

One of the first mantra's of ying/yang theory, "don't expect anything for nothing, and you'll never be disappointed". I would go so far as to say, "don't envy the rich, don't pity the poor", but that may be stretching in some cases. Charity begins at home, and what's left is a personal obligation to those who can serve and give their time and/or money to others truly in need, but it should never be forced upon the individual. I don't know where the lawyers will find the words that indicate the government and/or Constitution has the right to force these ideas on anyone.

March 26, 2010

There have been times in this country's history where there was no president, vice president and/or Congress in session or running (I first misspelled this to say "ruining", but I am certain that was a typo) things. I believe things ran rather smoothly. Check it out. Anyway, my point is that no, we probably cannot afford to run amok among the land trying to resolve every problem any which way the wind blows at that moment. However, the pendulum seems to have swung over to the point where if you're not part of a special interest, you ain't part of nuthin'. I believe I may have already mentioned the way to obtain a decent life is working for it, stop spending when you cannot, take the hits in the budget and move on. There will be pain. It's just a question of how much.

Countries that are now beginning to reap the benefits of our old ways (stay out of too much debt, keep rates realistic, not artificially low, become more self sufficient, union "bust up", at least a little), have a plan, stick to it and have a little faith that "the harder we work, the luckier we'll get".

March 30, 2010

I wait for an oil change, and lo' and behold, there has to be a week old newspaper in the empty seat next to me. I cannot believe how many times I read the very words I am or have thought about in the past and past along (mainly to Karen, an unsuspecting audience of one and even then, she probably tunes me out when I get too crazy here). The term, radical as it may seem, of impeachment comes to mind at times. To understand the constitutionality of what this process would imply is way beyond the scope of my understanding procedurally, but events governed by the executive and legislative branches of recent have stirred the pot to the point where you get tired of "just do it my way and someday you'll understand". These items, mainly health care related, with all its non-health care entitlement attachments, are too costly. The not-so-hidden agenda of these laws (why bother to hide it, they're gonna' do it anyway) are becoming more a pretext to a greater divide.

The constant barrages of items against the far left (I say far because being of fair minded left of center would have valid issues) are more than prevalent in this country's history. Yet when the real violence begins, you hardly hear a word or story of it from, what I would have to say these days, is a corrupt media. Most of these new agencies and print media suffer from declining audiences, revenues and sponsoring, and yet they continue to spew their rhetoric.

This is a progressive "pied-piper march" (another term I mentioned to K last year, only to see it on the cover of a US News and World Report story attached to caricature of Mr. Obama) to hell. Once again, the "lame stream media" (a borrowed term thanks to Bernie Goldberg) is fearful to say anything against a president for racial implications.

In previous scribbling, I mentioned this, and against, more insistently think this is another form of the racial reversal of our times. Who is really being racist? When you incite over as much change as has occurred in the last year or so, blame previous administrations for everything under the sun, take credit for things others who came before you (Iraq, one example, although we should leave, like….now), then who becomes responsible for setting back racial relations 50…60….70 years?

You begin to lay certain groundwork when you instill fear into the general populace. My mother-in-law and others like her have carried certain beliefs in their lifetime that may seem hard wired into their systems. It's what got them to the dance, so to speak. No shortcuts, no gimmies, no welfare. It's just long years of dedication to a purposeful life. However, when you can't (or won't) change your mind over logic because "I hate her voice" or "I could never vote for that younger or older guy", because you don't want someone to tell you some of your thought process may have been misguided.

Many of the individuals in this administration have too many ties to previous hard socialist to fascist to communist thinking. Under the guise of freedom, they strive for collective, "Borg" way of thinking, but for you, not them. It may be that I seem to be a racist because I do not aspire to think in Marxist, Maoist, Stalinist, Che-ist, ways, but hell, if anyone in outer space came to visit us, and spewed this way of thinking, i.e. "we are here to help",…sure you are. The earth would rise to the occasion, I would presume, to kick their space ball-asses back to where they came. Would that make us racist towards outer space folks?

April 25, 2010

Nothing inspires.

I am having breakfast out with Karen this morning. She says no more getting "upset" over current events before bedtime. I tell her it's not that I am getting upset, it just in the genuflection of my voice. She disagrees. Ok, so the health care, Iran/Iraq/Afghanistan, economy overall, Arizona border thing, Wall street/financial reform, taxes (part of economy) things have been overplayed, over done, etc.

I know, how about environmental issues? I never bought into the recycling/saving the planet thing. The earth will survive, no matter what we do to it, because ultimately we'll all be gone and it will still be here. Anyway, I let K know when the car finally poops out, and I am ready for the golf cart type next vehicle or bicycle, it will be because it is the change in my lifestyle, not the environment (subject to any God forbid mandating) that make the decision for me. On this issue, K gives me the point. I don't get many, so I'll take it. Maybe I will have this "luxury" but every generation says the same thing i.e. "I'm glad I am not young raising kids in this environment"…you ask your parents/grandparents. Ask you kids/grandkids…..it'll all sound the same, for different reasons obviously, but you get through it, somehow.

Just finished Mr. Dorsey's next to latest one, "Nuclear Jellyfish". I concluded the reading on a plane ride from New Jersey. Now there's a place in turmoil. The folks sitting around me must've thought I was nutty, cackling to myself. As I may have explained previously, these type of books aren't for everyone, but I lov'em. Even became a fan member, t-shirt, hat and all. I tracked the website when Mr. D. will be in the Keys again. You do your own homework there; it will be crowded enough. Got to get home and tend to the vegetable garden. Did I happen to mention I started another one? With K's guidance, it's really coming along, getting the peppers, tomatoes, various types of squash, "cuke's" and beans,…really enjoy it.

Yeah, life's getting simpler all the time.

May 3, 2010

So I have read about Denmark's conversion to move to more self sufficiently in recent years. This movement actually originated back in the seventies after the Arab oil embargo.

Denmark decided it was too dependent on too many others for their energy needs (you do the extensive reading) and now are an energy exporter in some areas. Now granted, there's only 5-6 million folks living there and (I assume) mostly homogeneous, but you get the picture. In their case, they raised taxes up the wazoo (the sales tax on a vehicle purchase is greater than the price of the vehicle itself, for example) but you know, if ya' use the money for its intended use and don't steal it or give it away to the precious few, it's a good example of how things can work . Granted, it may be more a nanny state than many of us would want, but it's still an example of an impressive accomplishment.

Sometimes, I think at a young age we get into a "save the world" mentality, which makes us more democratic (how this administration may have pulled it off). Then, as we get a little older, work hard for our means of support, try and save a little for the future, we tend to want to keep what we have reaped and sowed, which tends to make us more conservative. You aren't the ones a more liberal administration can change so they have to start over with young ones. Then you become a senior citizen and if they take it all away, you are faced with the government having to support you and end up democratic again. I hope not. Just a thought.

May 8, 2010

Sitting in the pool with K thinking, any given moment we think like socialists, liberals, democrats, republicans, conservatives, libertarians or citizens....I believe at any time we have these natural tendencies to do this, we're not god-like or deists, just people trying to survive or enjoy life. Go ahead, say you don't, see if I care, you hypocrite...no, matter, we go on. My, or should I say our goals have been set. My desire to live in the Keys, whether right or wrong is strong enough to work towards it. We will go from there.

May 10, 2010

We had some of the family over yesterday, swimming, enjoying and conversing. Saw a title to a movie the other day. Although I did not actually watch it, "The Magic of Ordinary Days" has a nice ring to it, as well as a lot of truth.

May 13, 2010

So Karen comes home a little late from a meeting, I am outside enjoying the view, a little whiskey and cigar in tow. I highlight the latest Glenn Beck episode I see, and then it's her turn about the day and I realize I didn't solve anything with the world or her situation at present, but the world kept on a' spinnin'...oh well, maybe tomorrow.

May 16, 2010

Had a conversation with an old friend via e-mail about the old days (our professions during our working time in our chosen field of endeavor). He actually hired me and went on to become the company's CEO. Anyway, a little reminiscing never hurt, but not too much lest it does. I suppose it's just another passage in life, these types of things we do and did. Still, it was interesting to note how things have changed and will continue to do so. The basic premise of lending (the profession) may be what is necessary for the continuance of the business, but how, who, where, when and why it's done will have its changing moments for all time. I will leave it at that.

May 17, 2010

So K is telling me she needed to use some hydrogen peroxide to cleanse a small wound she had to really get it cleaned out. It's really the best stuff. Like I always say, if you can't accomplish your goal with a hammer, duct tape or hydrogen peroxide, it can't be fixed.

May 22, 2010

"This time it's different". How many times do we have to listen to this statement about the financial markets? In spite of everything, I still believe in America. That is to mean, some of us will tend to overreact to dot-com bubbles, my "neighbor's brother's father-in-law's great uncle" who made a short term killing in the collateralized debt obligation market (i.e. the slot machine just worked right in "Lost Wages"), real estate bubbles, tech bubbles, etc. Look, if you absolutely need to know you have to walk around your house stubbing your toes on gold bars, go for it, but realize the consequences of too much hoarding. Ya' still got to sell it because you can't take it to Publix. I suppose it is a safe haven for those who can play the game.

The bottom line for most of us too moronic to know what to do is, well, nothing, or at least very, very little. Sways in the market come and go, and your broker advisor or the real one (the one between you ears) should be telling you to not panic. The only real difference this time is, well, you're a little older, maybe close to retirement or already there one way (forced) or the other, and you tend to believe the money's flying out the door faster than you'd like (I know, I have these thoughts).

Take it easy, talk to both of the aforementioned advisors above, especially the one between your ears. Ask yourself how you got to where you are in the first place, forgive yourself for past transgressions you may have thought you didn't like, believe in, etc. Keep it simple. Take simple steps, if any, to change the long term outlook (a little less in equities (stocks) and maybe a little more in long term security), albeit a lower rate of return. Chalk it all up to experience, ask yourself "am I going to go broke today?", then stop reading this gibberish, get away from the computer, go outside, take a deep breath......enjoy!!

June 3, 2010

I got a bad case of a sciatica nerve problem (as if there's a good case of one). Anyway, it's a real problem at times, especially at night. K's doing the best she can for me, but got to tough it out myself. I have had it before, but not this bad.

Watching the tube sure doesn't help to relax oneself when you're not whole, so maybe need to stay away from it a little more. Lot's of blaming going around on the oil spill matter, while livelihoods going away. The political maneuvering is rather, well...disgusting, but when is it ever not at least that adjective.

This sounds pretty lame, but I am actually waiting for the cable guy this morning. There supposed to check a weak line causing too much interruption of service (translation- the monthly bill's going north). In addition, can't get a tree company to call back for some high up branches to be cut, insurance squabbles over me overpaying on co-pays been going on for about four months, trying to find some "lost" stock mentions on the monthly statements.....in other words, just another day.

June 4, 2010

I heard from an old mentor in my business life through
Facebook yesterday. In fact, I get quite a few reminders of
the old days through this source. I do respond in kind but
kindly inform folks I prefer not to use a Facebook method of
communication. E-mails can be dangerous enough. Anyway,
I responded. He had placed a photograph of himself in the
Facebook page. He looked older than his years, but knowing
some of the history there, it does not surprise. On visiting us
in the Florida office one time many years back, he
commented, "Florida seems like a good place to retire
from"....I could never seem to forget those words, and in
light of recent events here (check the news of the day), they
may seem appropriate soon enough.

June 11, 2010

July 10, 2001- written what seems like so long ago.....

Here's our story
It's sad but true....
About a Company
That we once knew...

They took our loyalty
And ran amok....
With predetermined foresight

To tell us, hey! - Your outta' luck…

When it was all said
And done…
You were no better
Than any other corporate bum…

Just more lives shattered
And maligned…
To add to those
On the unemployment line…

But there is hope, and value and foresight
That there are others who will see…
That the future can still be bright
For folks such as we…

June 12, 2010

Our Mindless Ways

Driving to my destination,
I think the way of life we lead,
Too overcome with doubt and guilt,
To worry about the speed

It's a fragile situation,
Sometimes fraught with fears,

The Democrats only happy drilling into your wallet,
Republicans guilt trip you with god fearing ideas

Oh where, oh where has the money be gone,
While the masses keep paying the toll,
It's gone to a place unimagined by most,
A place you cannot go, into the black hole

But Dem's, Repub's, Commies, there all just labels,
Seem born with their preset list of instructions,
Only thing they tell themselves about us,
We can't think for ourselves, we're all self destructives

So you drive down that road to your mindless way,
Try to save the day and make a dollar,
Don't turn on that media dial,
'Lest you want to hear yourself holler

Oh where oh where has the money be gone,
While the masses keep paying the toll,
It's gone to a place unimagined by most,
A place you cannot go, into the black hole

Words like stimulus, tax evader and TARP,
All hypocrisies given to those who bark...
"We did it, took the dough and we'll take it again",
Just try and stop us from printing more Ben,

Tax the cap gains, tax the dead,

Keep buying those guns 'til Prop 2 takes one in the head,
Tax small business and three numbered plans,
Keep the joints burning, 'til the West Coast is out of the red,

You gotta' get with the program
And buy all the hype
Or your next govm'int hospital visit,
You may forever say good night

I'm really getting into the swing of nut ball thoughts between the ears sometimes, but no matter.....I just wish I could write some lyrics.....maybe someone out there can assist?

Government "assassins", why to we allow? Someone help us from these parasites and clowns. They are not stupid, just trying to constantly mislead, misdirect: they must love this oil spill thing...detracts from health care concerns, of which the writer has some issues himself. Anyway, maybe this fall we will take back at least some control of this insanity.

June 15, 2010

If you couldn't tell, I've been feeling a little in the "dark mood" lately. Got a little sciatica problem and it's lingering too long. Detracts from my thought processes. What can ya' do but go on. I wish it were just that, but too many other little things are adding up. It...shall....all...pass. This is not the time of our lives to be sad. Worked long and fairly hard at times to get this far, hate to blow it, but of course, not much control there. Lots of wolves at the door, looking for an easier ride than the one we've taken.

June 22, 2010

Can't tell the good guys from the bad, or maybe the not so good from the not so bad. No one's perfect. It's getting pretty hypocritical out there in this land of ours. I only hope we can survive it all. Still, sad.

Someone asked me about being "shitted on" earlier today. My definition of the term would be something like, when you do the right thing; you can still find yourself in the shitted on mode. Take the banks vs. the government, for example. Many banks did the right thing over the rough period of recent times. Now those banks are having the government force products, audits and "services" down their throats they neither want nor need. Of course the banks, fearing reprisals and retributions, tell decent loan candidates we cannot give you money because we have to account to the government for every nickel spent and everything we do. So while the bean counters take over (they are not profit centers, you know) with one hand, the other hand waves bye-bye to good business because of this narrow mindedness. The government's slight of hand is to blame all the banks for the problem while ignoring the real culprits, some greed at wall street level coupled with the fannie-freddie fiasco (note the spell check requests I capitalize "wall street" and "fannie-freddie"....I choose to ignore giving them proper names since of late, they do not deserve such statue). You do the right thing, and you watch these non-deserving proper names clobber you. Oh, and by the way, you banks, insurance agencies, brokerages and such who would continue to believe in a bail our for all the unwarranted risks they take....fuggedddaaaabouuutttttit......you succeed or fail on your own merits, oh know, I can't believe it....actually doing what you are supposed to do without some one else watching your back....

I believe I heard Barney Frank the other day speaking to some folks at a town hall type meeting or something say "he never saw a tax cut create a job" or something to that effect. You gotta' be kiddin' me.....because if you need an explanation of tax cuts doing more good than this spending spree of late, shame on you guys....they know it's wrong what they do, but who's gonna' stop'em? Next election better get them out or they'll keep kicking the can down the road knowing it won't be their problem. Even Europe's startin' to figure it out.....jeeeezzz, how much more hints do ya' need?

June 25, 2010

I get these thoughts in the middle of the night. I don't get up to jot them down. What I remember of them is something about the "spiritualness" of mankind. Not being a very religious person (borderline agnostic), there seemed to be a thought process of the more perfect situation of equalities of our species. Weird, I know. Anyway, it came and went, probably something to do with one of the books I am reading now, but it gave me a presence of mind to sleep a little better. Maybe hope for us yet, but we need to kill off the preferred professions in the legal and political world, or at least limit their effectiveness. No "'cumbayaing" here, just using more common sense would help. Never mind.

July 2, 2010

Been not feeling too great of late. The stock market's trying to take my simple life retirement away a little faster than I would like. These "power folks" cause the situation, but they don't share in the risk, then talk about cutting Social Security and the like. "Cork Sockers", all of 'em!!....I suppose you come into the world with nothing and you're probably going to leave the same way.

July 3, 2010

More bills to pay, more insurance denials, more surprises. It's amazing how much crap your roof has to go through when K wants more sun over the pool area by having trees cut back. Some of those branches hitting the roof scare the crap outta' you. I hope this ends today. Looked at the newspaper this morning....more of the same. There is some good things going on out there somewhere, but that doesn't sell print. As I may have mentioned, that method's going out of style anyway, but the computer sprouts the same rhetoric. Anyway, going to walk around outside now and see how much more I have to concern myself with when the next rains come.

July 13, 2010

What the hell is becoming of us? We must be crazy, or "I must have misspoken before, because what I meant to say was something else, but I reserve the right to go back to the misspoken words later, if it suites my (political) career".....

We are spending ourselves into oblivion......that's it....end of story....it won't change with the present situation. We have a new double standard in race relations. We allow "jacksonisms" (not Andrew, of course) to continually propel us backwards when the majority of us are a fair minded group......more quotes from news agencies about how we have all become socialists (uhhhh, speak for yourselves, please). Too many folks wanting a free ride.......ahhhh, well, another day....

July 14, 2010

I fear what could happen is exactly what the majority does not want to occur. A minority with no viable options but to play the race card will force the majority (which, probably own a whole lot more weapons) to make this all come to blows. The ends will seem to justify the means, and everything we did not want to happen (what the founders had to do, not us) will happen. What a shame on us. We let the tail wag the dog for their own power, money and control. Let the wealthiest of those sprouting the redistribution rhetoric be the first in line to divide their wealth amongst those they feel deserve your hard earned dough. Listening to these religious cuckoos and zealots, they should not have the air time.

July 17, 2010

Reading some interesting leads on latest books in the WS Journal about how countries viewed the fanaticisms of fascism, nazism and the like prior to war. Seems an interesting read or two. In the middle of some other books, and I would suggest the politicos read some of this stuff (i.e. history repeating itself) but hey, it they can't read the new laws being passed down (stuffed down) on us, why would they bother reading this stuff?

In addition, from Peggy Noonan about where the "old guys" went or are going in the business arena, as in retiring, being forced out, giving up, etc. It's too bad, but there are no heroes anymore, and before the "youngins" try to learn from the experienced ones (not necessarily always right but still have the understanding to analyze situations) they would rather force them out.

July 26, 2010

K and I took a short vacation south. I always love being in the Florida Keys, even think about spending more of my old age there. It will depend on several things, not the least of which is when Karen thinks she will leave the education field. She says a year or so, but the way things are going, if I were a betting man, it could be longer. We'll see. In any event, I did some brokering business last week which entitled me to a small fee. I am off to collect same this morning.

I have returned, with fee in the bank. A reasonable amount, fair to all parties concerned. While I am in profit motif, in the "so let me get this straight in my mind" scenario, two very profitable entities, our hospital group and our insurance company, cannot get along on how much of an increase one has to pay and one wants to keep to remain contractually obligated, so if they don't resolve soon, the losers are, well, let's see, hmmmm.....oh yes,....us. We get to not go to our primary care physician and have to begin looking for inconvenient ways to obtain health/hospital care. Way to go, present administration. As I age, I begin to feel the effects of....well, age. I hope they can agree soon, or it's more effort and more cost health wise. Did we really think it was going to be any other way?

July 29, 2010

No one has blinked yet on the aforementioned insurance scenario. In the meantime, cover of WSJ speaks of more Americans taking less insurance, or none, or plans with higher deductibles or less elective surgical procedures (like, you wanna' walk but you cannot afford to have your knees fixed). Way to go again, for the mainstream, present admin....keep lettin' those illegals get all the bennies while the folks who worked their whole lives, paid into the sys.....ahhhh, never mind, for another day. It's like Mr. Beck said yesterday, you smell smoke in the house, but the significant other says stop complaining about this stuff....diversionary tactics.

August 3, 2010

Still no word on the insurance...oh, well. I referred a customer to a third party for a finance deal and was paid a fee for same. I guess I am still in the game slightly, but not very much. It gives me too much time to review the state of affairs. That isn't always a good thing, unless you really want to get into it and can afford same. Fascists are everywhere. Remember, capitalism represents freedom....to fail, succeed, jump off a bridge ...anything that no one should be able to control.

August 6, 2010

I suppose someone will blink soon on insurance matters....thought about a "refi" on the house....the bank, which at one time was waaaayy too generous on valuing the house (back in the good old days of.....2006!!) now says goes too far the other way (in my humble opinion)....forget it, will live with the present situation, although it does give thought to my/our plight of where I may want to be in the next few years.

I am more in belief in the thought process that this government is going even further down the socialist/fascist line than I would have ever imagined. Academia with no thought other than what they have learned behind the walls taking credit for moving stimulus funds (that artificial money no one in real businesses ever gets to play with) to prop up entities whose time has come and need to be realigned or gone. Most of these folks haven't the slightest idea about creating something from their own blood, sweat and years of making something out of nothing with nothing much. I suppose it won't change in the near term but things will come to head soon enough.

August 10, 2010

It's reassessment time again. I am getting the feeling like congress must have these days. It's a sense of irrelevancy. No, this is not a "poor feel sorry for me" type thing. I would like to believe mostly that has not been an issue in my life (even though, as they say, if you don't feel a bit sorry for yourself once in a while, who will)?

No, this is more like, maybe we spent too much time talking and not listening. Current events are important, for it seems more than ever, they are going to shape this country over the course of the next several months, or years, or whatever timeframe you choose. My own feelings, after all the finger pointing and slamming each other, is everyone in power too long needs to go. Period. It doesn't matter if you did a good job or otherwise, it has to start over. A lot of us say this, then go listen to one person get the last word on television or has more signs cluttering the lawns around town, and well, we know what happens. Maybe this time it will be different. Maybe…...

…and, in the "you know" category, what if you ran or worked for a business that, no matter how inept it was, no matter how much money it lost, how many bad decisions management makes, no matter how much you over compensate for workers……you can never go out of business. Wouldn't you like to have a business like this?...Some wall street type outfits think they could do this and have, but you know what entity I speak of here…..come on, you know…….I cannot say you guessed correctly……you just know…..

August 11, 2010

So, now that you have figured it out, how much more socialism can you stand? We have folks on the government payroll making (earning?) incredible amounts of money after they leave the service, all having to be paid through private sector taxation. The very elite will move their money elsewhere, leaving us to pay for this ballooning deficit. Most states in trouble only have to look at their own situations to realize what they have done. All the marijuana sales in the world won't offset their deficits, so they have to keep sucking it out of the real innovators (small businesses) to keep their schemes a'flowin'

Big business and big government....not a good recipe if you are the working class. November is coming, so we'll see what folks mean by change.

There are too many people claiming to be victims these days. I saw a commercial the other day where a retired sports figure that had spent time in court for doing, shall we say, wrong things, was back doing said commercial. Without sounding too prudish, what kind of message is being sent to young ones (and not so young ones) about what happens when you do things that should land you in jail and not back on TV?

I know most of us will not go out and do illegal or eventful things which will draw the wrong attention to themselves, but this kind of behavior's getting pretty old and if you need this as a source of news, at least make the punishment fit the crime, no?

August 17, 2010

So, I wonder how many of us know how many tax laws are really going to change next year. I happened to see a list from an associate through the e-mail. No wonder it didn't matter who read the bills. It was chuck full of increases from paying more for your health care (it won't cost you one red cent, or dime more, someone said in a speech not too long ago) to pre-taxing the health spending accounts again (why have them if there's no tax benefit) to more AMT qualifiers. You name it, it's going up. It's bad enough it's going up, but what's worse is what those SOB's in congress will do with the money. Not apply it to deficits, not stabilize Social Security or Medicare. What a waste. It's not that the leader is or isn't an American citizen. It's that he and they do un-American things!!

Pull the Constitution out whenever it suits your needs. "Negative liberties"....what the hell is that all about?....Tolerance, from everyone but those who should be the more tolerant....it's pretty disguising out there, and November better mean something to us, or it's off to another land for those who would like to make a difference here, and I don't blame them. No one lives forever; no one gets out alive.....

August 18, 2010

The "Doctor" speaks:

On real estate: I drove by a couple of recently built large homes in the area today and noticed "for sale" signs. Interesting, you know, because these homes seemed large enough in the first place a few years ago, and now, after whomever bought the homes tore them down to build larger ones, must find themselves in one hell of a pickle. "The Doctor's lesson in real estate; if you're not into it as a profession and/or up to your eye sockets in this business, i.e., you put your life's blood, sweat and tears on the line, not to mention (although I am mentioning) you a--...what the f... are you doing and who are you trying to impress? People in the business "time the market" when things are great and tell you to buy when things suck because that's when things are slow and low pricewise, but they cannot truly be perfect when it all time's itself, and they are the professionals, so how the hell can you time it?

On personal finance: On this Doctor is particularly keen, since it is near and dear to what's left of his heart. Let's say you worked for thirty/forty years or so and were able, in spite of kids, cars, homes, educations and the untold expenses in life, to rack up a 500M savings nest egg. The number itself may be unimportant, could be much higher or lower, but I use it for clarity. The point is you saved something besides waiting for your social security check.

Anyway, this 500M, after the last couple of years of "fun in the marketplace", has dwindled to say, 300M, depending on your tolerance for risk these days. I hear mostly everyone has trusted or has a trusted source somewhere, but risk is inherent, especially since we know what a flip of the wrong switch can do to all those nickels and dimes.

You've lost 30-40% of your portfolio in a period of time so narrow. Unless you know people, when you see these financial repair type guys, financial institutions "feel your pain" to get back on track, the Doctor asks, how the hell can anybody promise you to get back to where you were two years ago? It took you all those years to earn it, not so many years to lose a good chunk of it, so now you're gonna' risk it again to get back to where you belong? You'll be long gone (barring Publisher's Clearing House knocking on your door) before you recover. The fact is, unless you pulled out waaaaaaay early on the Bernie Madoff syndrome, get used to it. Why would you risk the rest, I don't know, but hopefully things will at least stabilize.

<u>On race relations:</u> Probably one of the biggest scams of all. This is a great country. I did not say a perfect one, but over time, I believe we learn from errors, albeit slowly at times, in history. To criticize a leader because of skin color is ludicrous in any free thinking society, and if the only attack you have against me is you're picking on someone because of skin color, you need to recheck yourself. The Doctor says why would we be having an intelligent conversation about the state of the nation's problem and some one talk

unintelligently about race? If that happens, then we cannot have an intelligent conversation and we should cease talking. Do most free thinking decent people really see color when it comes to opening your health care bill (assuming you have health care) to see a larger bill? Do we see color when taxes go up and these increases don't solve the reason for said increase? Do we see color when our military gets crapped on and everyone has to be tolerant of those who won't tolerate us?

Maybe we do see color and it's red. I hope we don't just get angry, I hope folks a whole lot smarter than me do what is necessary to stop the blaming and start the retaining of people who will right the present course. I try to do my part at times, but these moments for me are fleeting, and that is a fault I am trying to overcome.

Anyway, these are the Doctor's opinions, and he's sticking to'em.

August 22, 2010

"Yeah, I'm the Rate adjustment man, yeaaaaah; I'm the Rate Adjustment maaaaaannnn.....somehow, doesn't have the same ring to it, does it? (Beatles, "Taxman" song, for those of you who didn't get my drift here).

So, this business model of capitalism doesn't work, eh? You're right, if government steps in too much to prop up businesses and you stay in bed with them for any length of time. Ask yourself this; if businesses such as a World Com, or Enron can't keep their doors open because it was time for them to fail, then why shouldn't more businesses follow suit?

Governments which think we should constantly spend our selves out of these situations, in the writer's opinion, seem to have it backwards. When governments reduce taxes across the board, they take a little less from a much wider base. People and businesses may seem more willing to pay their share if they know it's not a punishing situation with no end in sight. Instead, a government says, we'll raise taxes (adjustments, reapportionments, recalibrations, call'em what you want) on all, hopeful that folks will think it still will only affect a minority of folks at the upper echelons. By doing this, however, it causes stagnation in employment opportunities, cost effectiveness to the bottom line; no confidence in future tax "adjustments" and things such as health....i.e. no one invests.

Let's face it, the very wealthy move with these situations to havens most others cannot, leaving the burden on the working class. Reducing the working class reduces the amount of taxes which can be collected and, geeez....we know these things.

August 24, 2010

K. says I should consider putting this entire dribble through publishing with an Amazon or something similar. I don't know...I believe it was Nietzsche who said "the best author is the one who is ashamed to become a writer"...maybe not so much ashamed as the just knowing these were my notes, things I could say in short, simplified ways to read later and reflect, or enjoy or wonder how the hell I think of these things. She does understand my fear, though.

August 25, 2010

At this point, I feel enough is being spewed through all the media outlets on both sides of the aisle and those in the middle to let these writings rest, at least until we see what occurs after the elections.

I don't know what will occur henceforth, nor do I have any suspicions about life going through dramatic changes in either direction. Already we are seeing candidates arguments slandering the hell out of each other...it gets old. Maybe that's the whole idea...it gets old, people end up not caring because they're worn down from the same old rhetoric.

Are we looking for heroes, or are we seeing more of the same to accept the (lesser?) acts of those who would at least appear to do us the least harm. We shall see. I suppose much of this information is stored in many of us, and did you ever notice how some people can express themselves in such a way like someone took the ideas right out of your head? You thought it, they said it, and maybe more folks listen to those who get more than their fifteen minutes.

No matter what, I wish everyone well and the best they can be. As I mentioned at the start, tomorrow may be promised to no one, but hopefully those in charge will make life a little easier along the way. Ultimately, I believe that job is left to us all.